Sell Smarter, Not Harder

The Ultimate Guide To Sales Success
Jules Beshears

Copyright © 2023 by Jules Beshears / 414 Industries

All rights reserved.

No portion of this book may be reproduced in any form without written permission from the publisher or author, except as permitted by U.S. copyright law.

Contents

Message From The Author 1
1. Introduction to Marketing and Sales 2
2. Understanding Your Target Audience 4
3. Developing a Marketing Strategy 7
4. Building a Strong Brand Identity 11
5. Creating Effective Marketing Materials 14
6. Leveraging Social Media for Marketing 17
7. Content Marketing for Lead Generation 20
8. Email Marketing for Customer Engagement 23
9. Search Engine Optimization (SEO) for Increased Visibility 26
10. Pay-Per-Click (PPC) Advertising for Lead Generation 29
11. Influencer Marketing 33
12. Event Marketing for Lead Generation 37
13. Trade Show Marketing 40
14. Direct Mail Marketing 43
15. Telemarketing and Cold Calling Techniques 47
16. Sales Funnel Management 50
17. Closing Techniques for Sales 53
18. Building and Maintaining Customer Relationships 56
19. Measuring and Analyzing Marketing and Sales Performance ... 59
20. Staying Up-to-Date with Marketing and Sales Trends 63

1.
2.
3.
4.
5.
6.
7.
8.
9.
10.
11.

12.
13.
14.
15.
16.
17.
18.
19.
20.

Message From The Author

"Iwas told we are paid for our value and not our time." As such, my books, on the surface, may seem somewhat lacking in terms of page count. What they lack in the sheer number of pages that tell stories about me growing up, or making my first million, etc., I choose to prioritize value. The books I write remove most of the fluff and are condensed, distilled, raw value that will hopefully change your life for the better.

This book is dedicated to my family, friends, and to all the entrepreneurs that chose never to give up.

Chapter 1

Introduction to Marketing and Sales

Marketing and sales are two of the most critical aspects of any business. Marketing is the process of creating and promoting a product or service to potential customers, while sales involve converting those potential customers into actual buyers.

Marketing and sales are often viewed as separate entities, but they are profoundly interconnected and rely on each other to be effective. Marketing sets the stage for sales by attracting the right audience and building a positive image for the product or service. Sales, in turn, takes that marketing foundation and converts it into substantial revenue for the business.

In this book, we will explore the fundamental principles and tactics of marketing and sales and show you how to put them into action to drive growth for your business. Whether you're an entrepreneur starting a new venture or a sales professional looking to improve your performance, the insights and strategies in this book will help you succeed.

Together, marketing and sales form the foundation of a successful business, and a strong understanding of both is essential to long-term success. So let's dive in and start learning!

The world of marketing and sales is constantly changing, with new technologies and trends always emerging. However, at the core of both disciplines are some fundamental principles that have remained unchanged for decades. In this chapter, we will explore these principles and help you gain a solid understanding of the basics of marketing and sales.

You'll learn about the different types of marketing, including traditional marketing, digital marketing, and relationship marketing. You'll also discover the various channels and methods used to reach customers, such as advertising, public relations, and direct marketing.

We'll also cover the different stages of the sales process, including prospecting, qualification, presentation, handling objections, and closing. You'll learn the importance of establishing trust and rapport with your customers and using different sales techniques and strategies to close more deals.

By the end of this chapter, you'll have a comprehensive understanding of the basic concepts and principles of marketing and sales and be ready to dive deeper into the specific tactics and strategies in the following chapters. Whether you're new to marketing and sales or you've been in the game for a while, this chapter will provide you with the foundation you need to succeed.

Chapter 2

Understanding Your Target Audience

Understanding your target audience is one of the most critical steps in the marketing and sales process. Your target audience is the people most likely interested in your product or service and who you want to reach with your marketing efforts.

Knowing your target audience is crucial because it allows you to tailor your marketing and sales messages to their specific needs, interests, and pain points. This, in turn, makes your marketing more effective and your sales more efficient.

This chapter will cover the basics of target audience research and help you understand how to identify, segment, and reach your target audience.

Identifying Your Target Audience

The first step in understanding your target audience is identifying who they are. This involves analyzing demographic information, such as age, gender, income, education, and location. You can also look at psychographic information, such as values, attitudes, and lifestyles.

You can use several tools and techniques to gather this information, such as surveys, focus groups, and online analytics tools. You can also use existing market research data or collect information from your existing customers.

Segmenting Your Target Audience

Once you understand your target audience, you can segment them into smaller, more manageable groups. This allows you to tailor your marketing and sales messages to each group's specific needs and makes reaching them more straightforward with your marketing efforts.

For example, you might segment your target audience by age, with different marketing messages for different age groups. Or you might segment by location, with different marketing messages for customers in different regions.

Reaching Your Target Audience

Once you understand your target audience and have segmented them into smaller groups, it's time to reach out to them. This involves choosing the proper marketing channels to reach each group and creating marketing messages that resonate with them.

For example, you can reach younger customers through social media and influencer marketing, while older customers are more receptive to direct mail or print advertising.

It's important to remember that different groups within your target audience might respond to other marketing channels and messages. That's why it's essential to test and iterate your marketing efforts over time and to be flexible and adaptable in your approach.

Another critical aspect of understanding your target audience is understanding their pain points and motivations. What are the problems or challenges they are facing that your product or service can help solve? What motivates them to make a purchase? Understanding these factors will help you create messaging that speaks directly to your target audience and resonates with them.

It's also important to understand the customer journey of your target audience. How do they discover your product or service? What steps do they take before making a purchase? Understanding this journey can help you create a more effective marketing and sales strategy and ensure that your target audience receives the right messages at the right time.

Another aspect to consider is the buying behavior of your target audience. Are they price-sensitive? Do they prefer to purchase online or in-store? Understanding your target audience's buying behavior can help you create a more effective pricing strategy and choose the proper channels for reaching them.

Finally, monitoring and adjusting your target audience research over time is essential. As your target audience evolves and changes, so should your understanding of them. Regularly updating your research will ensure that your marketing and sales efforts remain effective and relevant.

In summary, understanding your target audience is an ongoing process that requires research, analysis, and adaptation. By taking the time to understand your target audience, you'll be able to create marketing and sales messages that resonate with them and ultimately drive more sales for your business.

Chapter 3

Developing a Marketing Strategy

Once you deeply understand your target audience, the next step is to develop a marketing strategy that reaches and resonates with them. A marketing strategy is a comprehensive plan for reaching your target audience and achieving your marketing goals.

In this chapter, we'll cover the key components of a marketing strategy and help you create a plan that works for your business.

Defining Your Marketing Goals

The first step in developing a marketing strategy is to define your marketing goals. What do you want to achieve through your marketing efforts? This could be increasing brand awareness, driving website traffic, generating leads, or increasing sales.

Once you have defined your marketing goals, you can use them to guide the rest of your marketing strategy. For example, if your goal is to increase brand awareness, you might focus on creating more engaging social media content. If your goal is to drive website traffic, you might invest in search engine optimization or pay-per-click advertising.

Choosing the Right Marketing Channels

The next step is to choose the proper marketing channels to reach your target audience. There are many marketing channels, including social media, email marketing, content marketing, search engine optimization, and paid advertising.

The proper marketing channels for your business will depend on your target audience, marketing goals, and budget. For example, if your target audience is active on social media, then social media marketing might be a good choice. If your target audience responds well to email marketing, that might be a better choice.

Creating a Content Marketing Plan

Content marketing is a powerful way to reach your target audience, build trust, and drive sales. It involves creating content that provides value to your target audience, such as blog posts, infographics, videos, and ebooks.

To create a content marketing plan, you'll need to define your goals, choose the correct content formats, and develop a content calendar. You'll also need to consider promoting your content and getting it in front of your target audience.

Implementing Your Marketing Strategy

Once you have developed your marketing strategy, it's time to implement it. This involves executing your marketing plan, tracking your results, and making necessary adjustments.

To ensure that your marketing strategy is effective, it's important to set up the correct tracking and analytics tools and to regularly review your results. This will help you understand what's working and what's not and make necessary adjustments.

It's also important to be flexible and adaptable in your approach. Your marketing strategy should evolve as your target audience, and the market evolves. Be open to changing and experimenting with new tactics to keep your marketing efforts effective and relevant.

Designing a Marketing Budget

Once you clearly understand your marketing goals and the channels you want to use to reach your target audience, the next step is to design a marketing budget. A marketing budget is a plan for how you'll allocate your resources to achieve your marketing goals.

To design a marketing budget, you'll need to consider the costs of each marketing channel and how much you're willing to invest in each one. For example, social media marketing may be relatively low, while paid advertising can be more expensive.

It's important to be realistic when designing your marketing budget. Consider the available resources, and make sure your budget is feasible. Don't over-extend yourself and try to do too much with too few resources, as this will impact the quality of your marketing efforts.

Measuring and Analyzing Your Marketing Results

To understand the effectiveness of your marketing strategy, you'll need to measure and analyze your results. This involves tracking key metrics, such as website traffic, conversions, and sales.

Various tools and technologies are available to help you track your marketing results. For example, Google Analytics is a powerful tool for tracking website traffic and conversions, while social media analytics tools can help you track engagement on social media.

By regularly measuring and analyzing your results, you'll be able to understand what's working and what's not and make any necessary adjustments to your marketing strategy.

Integrating Sales and Marketing

A vital component of a successful marketing and sales strategy is integration. Marketing and sales should work together as a unified team with a clear understanding of each other's goals and objectives.

For example, sales should provide marketing with insights into what's working and what's not so that marketing can make the necessary adjustments to its strategy. Marketing should also provide sales with the right tools and resources to help them close deals more effectively.

Integrating sales and marketing can lead to greater efficiency, better alignment, and more effective marketing and sales efforts.

Conclusion

Developing a marketing strategy is a crucial step in the marketing and sales process. By defining your marketing goals, choosing the proper marketing channels, and creating a content marketing plan, you'll be well on your way to reaching your target audience and achieving your marketing goals. With the right marketing strategy in place, you'll be able to drive more sales and grow your business.

Remember, marketing and sales are ongoing processes that require continuous improvement and adaptation. Be open to experimenting with new tactics, and regularly measure and analyze your results to ensure that your marketing strategy is effective and relevant.

Chapter 4

Building a Strong Brand Identity

Your brand identity is how you present yourself to the world. Your logo, messaging, tone of voice, and visual elements make up your brand image. A strong brand identity is crucial for attracting and retaining customers and establishing trust and credibility in your industry.

Why is Brand Identity Important?

Your brand identity helps you stand out from the competition and differentiate yourself from others in your industry. It also allows you to communicate your unique value proposition, and the benefits of your products or services, to potential customers.

Having a strong brand identity also builds trust and credibility with your customers. A well-designed brand identity conveys professionalism, competence, and a commitment to quality, which can help you create long-lasting relationships with your customers.

Components of Brand Identity

There are several key components of a strong brand identity, including:

1. Logo: Your logo is the visual representation of your brand and should be simple, memorable, and easily recognizable.
2. Messaging: Your messaging should clearly and concisely communicate the benefits of your products or services and what sets you apart from the competition.

3. The tone of Voice: Your tone of voice should be consistent across all of your marketing materials and should reflect your brand personality and values.
4. Visual Elements: Your visual elements, such as your color palette and typography, should be consistent across all your marketing materials and reflect your brand personality and values.

Building a Strong Brand Identity

1. Define Your Brand Personality: Before designing your brand identity, you must understand your brand personality. What values does your brand embody? What personality traits does your brand have? By defining your brand personality, you'll clearly understand the tone and style you want to convey in your brand identity.
2. Conduct Competitor Research: Understanding your competition is crucial for developing a solid brand identity that sets you apart from others in your industry. Study the brands in your industry, and analyze their brand identities, messaging, and marketing materials to understand what works and what doesn't.
3. Develop a Visual Identity: Your visual identity should reflect your brand personality and values and be consistent across all your marketing materials. This includes your logo, color palette, typography, and imagery.
4. Define Your Messaging: Your messaging should clearly and concisely communicate the benefits of your products or services and what sets you apart from the competition.

Develop a tagline or mission statement that summarizes your brand promise.
5. Create a Brand Style Guide: A brand style guide is a document that outlines the key elements of your brand identity, including your visual elements, messaging, and tone of voice. All members of your team should use this guide to ensure consistency in your brand identity across all marketing materials.

Building a strong brand identity is crucial for attracting and retaining customers and establishing trust and credibility in your industry. By defining your brand personality, conducting competitor research, developing a visual identity, and creating a brand style guide, you'll have a solid foundation for a strong brand identity that will help you grow your business.

Remember, your brand identity is ongoing and should evolve as your business grows and evolves. Be open to making changes and updates to your brand identity as necessary to keep it relevant and effective.

Chapter 5

Creating Effective Marketing Materials

Marketing materials are the tools you use to communicate your brand and promote your products or services to potential customers. Effective marketing materials should be visually appealing, easy to understand, and share your unique value proposition.

Types of Marketing Materials

1. Brochures: Brochures are an effective way to provide detailed information about your products or services and can be used as a leave-behind after a sales presentation or as a mailer to potential customers.
2. Business Cards: Business cards are a simple yet effective way to provide potential customers with your contact information and a summary of your products or services.
3. Direct Mail: Direct mail is a targeted, cost-effective way to reach potential customers through the mail. Direct mail can promote new products or services or introduce your business to a new audience.
4. Email Marketing: Email marketing is an effective way to reach potential customers directly in their inboxes. Email marketing can promote new products or services or keep your customers informed about your business.
5. Social Media: Social media is a powerful tool for reaching potential customers and building brand awareness. Social

media can promote your products or services or engage with your customers in real-time.

Tips for Creating Effective Marketing Materials

1. Know Your Target Audience: Understanding your target audience is crucial for creating effective marketing materials that resonate with your customers. Consider their needs, interests, and pain points, and use this information to inform the design and messaging of your marketing materials.

2. Use Clear and Concise Messaging: Make sure your marketing materials are easy to understand and convey a clear message. Avoid using industry jargon or technical language that your target audience may not be familiar with.

3. Focus on Benefits, Not Features: When promoting your products or services, focus on the benefits they offer your customers rather than just listing their features. This will help your customers see the value in your offering and make it more appealing to them.

4. Make it Visually Appealing: Use eye-catching design elements, such as color, images, and graphics, to make your marketing materials visually appealing. This will help capture the attention of your target audience and make your marketing materials more memorable.

5. Use Consistent Branding: Ensure your marketing materials are consistent with your overall brand identity. Use the same color palette, font, and logo across your marketing materials to create a consistent look and feel.

6. Test and Refine: Continuously test and refine your marketing materials to see what works best. Use metrics such as open rates, click-through rates, and conversion rates to measure the effectiveness of your marketing materials and make changes as needed to improve their performance.

Creating effective marketing materials is vital to your overall marketing and sales strategy. By understanding your target audience, using clear and concise messaging, and making your marketing materials visually appealing, you can help ensure that your materials effectively promote your products or services and build your brand.

Chapter 6

Leveraging Social Media for Marketing

Social media has become an integral part of modern life and offers a valuable opportunity for businesses to connect with their target audience. By leveraging social media for marketing, businesses can reach millions of potential customers and build brand awareness cost-effectively and engagingly.

Benefits of Using Social Media for Marketing

1. Increased Reach: Social media platforms have billions of active users, which allows businesses to reach a large and diverse audience.
2. Cost-Effective: Compared to traditional forms of advertising, social media marketing is relatively inexpensive and offers a high return on investment.
3. Real-Time Engagement: Social media allows businesses to engage with their audience in real time, which can help build brand loyalty and establish a relationship with customers.
4. Targeted Advertising: Social media platforms offer powerful targeting options, allowing businesses to reach their target audience precisely and efficiently.
5. Measurable Results: Social media platforms offer detailed analytics, which makes it easy to measure the success of your marketing campaigns and make data-driven decisions.

Strategies for Success on Social Media

1. Define Your Goals: Before starting your social media marketing campaign, it's essential to define your goals and understand what you hope to achieve. This will help guide your strategy and ensure that your efforts are focused and effective.
2. Choose the Right Platforms: Not all social media platforms are created equal. Choosing the most relevant platforms for your target audience and aligning them with your business goals is essential.
3. Develop a Content Strategy: A strong content strategy is essential for success on social media. Plan what type of content you will post, how often you will post, and what your tone and voice will be.
4. Engage With Your Audience: Social media is a two-way conversation. Make sure to engage with your audience by responding to comments, asking questions, and encouraging discussion.
5. Utilize Video Content: Video content is highly engaging and can help increase reach and engagement on social media. Consider incorporating video content into your social media strategy.
6. Measure and Refine: Continuously measure the results of your social media marketing efforts and make changes as needed to improve performance.
7. Collaborate with Influencers: Collaborating with influencers can be a great way to reach a new and broader audience. Consider partnering with influencers in your industry who

align with your brand values and can help promote your products or services to their followers.
8. Take Advantage of Advertising Opportunities: Many social media platforms offer advertising opportunities to effectively reach your target audience. Consider investing in paid advertising campaigns to reach a wider audience and drive more traffic to your website.
9. Utilize User-Generated Content: Encouraging your customers to share their experiences with your brand on social media can be a powerful marketing tool. Consider running campaigns or contests that encourage customers to share photos or stories related to your brand.
10. Stay Up-to-Date: The world of social media is constantly changing. Stay up-to-date with the latest trends and features on your platforms, and make changes to your strategy as needed to stay ahead of the curve.

Businesses can use many strategies and tactics to succeed on social media. By leveraging the power of social media for marketing, businesses can connect with their target audience, build brand awareness, and drive business growth in a cost-effective and engaging way. By following these strategies and continually measuring and refining your efforts, you can achieve success on social media and take your marketing to the next level.

Chapter 7

Content Marketing for Lead Generation

Content marketing is a strategic approach to creating and distributing valuable, relevant, and consistent content to attract and retain a clearly defined target audience — to drive profitable customer action. When it comes to lead generation, content marketing can be an incredibly effective tool for attracting and nurturing potential customers.

Benefits of Content Marketing for Lead Generation

1. Attracting Targeted Traffic: By creating high-quality, relevant content, businesses can attract a targeted audience interested in their products or services.
2. Building Trust and Authority: By consistently delivering valuable and relevant content, businesses can establish themselves as a trusted authority in their industry, which can help build trust with potential customers.
3. Nurturing Leads: Content marketing allows businesses to provide potential customers with the information they need to make informed decisions, helping to move them through the sales funnel and closer to making a purchase.
4. Cost-Effective: Compared to traditional forms of advertising, content marketing can be more cost-effective and offer a high return on investment over the long term.

Strategies for Effective Content Marketing for Lead Generation

1. Know Your Target Audience: Understanding your target audience is key to creating content that will attract and engage them. Consider their needs, challenges, and interests when creating content.
2. Define Your Goals: Clearly defining your goals for your content marketing efforts will help guide your strategy and ensure that your efforts are focused and effective.
3. Create a Content Plan: Developing a content plan will help ensure that you consistently create and distribute relevant and valuable content to your target audience.
4. Utilize a Variety of Content Types: Different types of content can be effective for different sales funnel stages. Consider using a mix of blog posts, ebooks, infographics, videos, and more to reach your target audience in various ways.
5. Optimize for Search Engines: Ensuring your content is optimized for search engines can help improve visibility and attract more targeted traffic to your website.
6. Use Calls-to-Action: Including calls-to-action in your content can help encourage potential customers to take the next step in the sales process.
7. Measure and Refine: Continuously measure the results of your content marketing efforts and make changes as needed to improve performance.
8. Collaborate with Influencers and Other Businesses: Collaborating with influencers and other businesses can help you reach a new and wider audience. Consider partnering with influencers in your industry or companies that complement

your offerings to promote your content and reach a new audience.

9. Repurpose Your Content: Don't let your content go to waste. Consider repurposing your content into different formats, such as turning a blog post into a video or an infographic. This will allow you to reach different audiences and maximize the impact of your content.

10. Engage with Your Audience: Engaging with your audience through comments, social media, and email is a great way to build relationships and increase brand loyalty. Respond to comments and questions, and encourage your audience to share their thoughts and feedback.

11. Invest in Content Promotion: While creating high-quality content is important, it's equally important to promote it effectively. Consider investing in content promotion through social media, email marketing, and other channels to drive traffic and reach your target audience.

Content marketing is a powerful tool for lead generation that can help you attract and engage potential customers, build trust and authority, and drive business growth. By following these strategies and continually refining your efforts, you can succeed with your content marketing efforts and achieve your lead generation goals.

Chapter 8

Email Marketing for Customer Engagement

Email marketing is a cost-effective and highly targeted method of reaching potential and existing customers with personalized messages and offers. When executed correctly, email marketing can be a powerful tool for engaging with customers and building relationships that drive business growth.

Benefits of Email Marketing for Customer Engagement

1. Cost-Effective: Unlike other forms of marketing, email marketing is relatively low-cost, making it a cost-effective option for businesses of all sizes.
2. High Reach: With billions of email users globally, email marketing allows businesses to reach a large audience quickly and easily.
3. Personalized and Targeted: Email marketing allows businesses to personalize messages and target specific audience segments based on their behavior, interests, and more.
4. Measurable Results: Email marketing provides businesses with a wealth of data and insights that can help them track their success and improve their efforts over time.

Strategies for Effective Email Marketing for Customer Engagement

1. Know Your Target Audience: Understanding your target audience is key to creating effective email marketing campaigns. Consider their interests, behaviors, and needs when creating your campaigns.
2. Segment Your List: Segmenting your email list based on behavior and interests can help you send more targeted and personalized messages to your audience.
3. Create Compelling Subject Lines: Your subject line is often the first thing your audience will see, so it's important to create subject lines that are compelling and relevant and entice your audience to open your email.
4. Use a Clear Call-to-Action: Including a clear and specific call-to-action in your email can help drive engagement and encourage your audience to take action.
5. Optimize for Mobile: With more and more people accessing their email on mobile devices, optimizing your emails for mobile viewing ensures they look great and are easy to read on any device.
6. Test and Refine: Continuously testing and refining your email marketing efforts can help you improve your results and drive engagement with your audience.
7. Automate Your Emails: Automating your email marketing efforts can help you save time and effort while providing a more personalized and consistent experience for your audience.
8. Incorporate Personalization: Personalizing your emails with the recipient's name, location, or past purchase history can

help increase engagement and make your emails feel more relevant and valuable to your audience.
9. Use A/B Testing: A/B testing allows you to test different elements of your emails, such as subject lines, calls-to-action, and more, to determine what works best and optimize your results.
10. Create a Sense of Urgency: Incorporating a sense of urgency in your emails, such as limited-time offers or exclusive access, can encourage your audience to take action quickly.
11. Build Relationships: Email marketing is a great way to build relationships with your audience by providing valuable content, offering exclusive access, and more. Consistently engaging with your audience through email can help you build trust and establish a loyal following.
12. Comply with Email Marketing Regulations: It's important to comply with email marketing regulations such as CAN-SPAM and GDPR to ensure that your emails are legal and ethical.

In summary, email marketing is an effective tool for customer engagement that allows businesses to reach their audience with personalized and targeted messages. By following these strategies and continually refining your efforts, you can achieve success with your email marketing campaigns and drive customer engagement.

Chapter 9

Search Engine Optimization (SEO) for Increased Visibility

Search Engine Optimization (SEO) is optimizing your website and online content to increase its visibility and ranking on search engines such as Google, Bing, and Yahoo. When executed correctly, SEO can help you attract more organic traffic to your website, increase brand visibility, and drive more leads and sales.

Why is SEO Important for Increased Visibility?

1. Increased Traffic: By ranking higher on search engines, you can attract more organic traffic to your website, which can help you increase your reach and exposure.
2. Improved User Experience: By optimizing your website for search engines, you can improve the user experience for your visitors by making it easier to navigate and find the information they need.
3. Increased Credibility and Trust: Ranking higher on search engines can increase your credibility and trust in the eyes of your audience, helping to build your brand and establish your business as a leader in your industry.
4. Cost-Effective: Unlike paid advertising, SEO is a cost-effective way to increase your visibility and reach, making it a great option for businesses of all sizes.

Strategies for Effective SEO for Increased Visibility

1. Conduct Keyword Research: Keyword research is identifying the keywords and phrases your target audience uses to search for your products or services. Conducting keyword research can help you optimize your website and content for the right keywords and phrases, increasing your visibility and ranking on search engines.
2. Create High-Quality Content: Creating high-quality, relevant, and useful content optimized for search engines is essential for increasing visibility and ranking.
3. Optimize Your Website Structure: The structure of your website, including headings, subheadings, and internal links, can impact your visibility and ranking on search engines. Make sure your website is well-structured and easy to navigate.
4. Use Meta Descriptions: Meta descriptions are short descriptions that appear below your page title in search engine results. Writing clear and compelling meta descriptions can help increase your click-through rates and drive more traffic to your website.
5. Optimize for Mobile: With most of the internet traffic now coming from mobile devices, optimizing your website for mobile to ensure that it is easy to use and navigate on any device.
6. Build Backlinks: Backlinks are links from other websites that point to your website. Building high-quality backlinks from reputable websites can help increase your visibility and ranking on search engines.

7. Track Your Results: Monitoring your SEO and tracking your results can help you make informed decisions about where to focus your efforts and what strategies work best for your business.

Chapter 10

Pay-Per-Click (PPC) Advertising for Lead Generation

Pay-Per-Click (PPC) advertising is a form of digital advertising where you pay each time a user clicks on one of your ads. PPC advertising allows you to target specific audiences and reach them with highly relevant ads at the right time, making it a powerful tool for lead generation.

Why is PPC Advertising Important for Lead Generation?

1. Targeted Advertising: PPC advertising allows you to target specific audiences based on geographic location, interests, and behaviors, making it a highly effective tool for reaching the right people at the right time.
2. Quick Results: Unlike SEO, which can take time to see results, PPC advertising can provide quick results and a high return on investment.
3. Increased Visibility: By appearing at the top of search engine results, PPC advertising can help increase your visibility and exposure to potential customers.
4. Measurable Results: PPC advertising provides measurable results, allowing you to track your return on investment and make informed decisions about your advertising budget and strategies.

Strategies for Effective PPC Advertising for Lead Generation

1. Define Your Target Audience: Understanding your target audience is key to creating effective PPC advertising campaigns. Define your target audience based on geographic location, interests, and behaviors.
2. Conduct Keyword Research: Keyword research is an essential part of PPC advertising. It helps you identify the keywords and phrases your target audience uses to search for your products or services.
3. Create Compelling Ad Copy: Creating compelling ad copy is essential for making your PPC ads stand out and attract clicks. Write clear, concise, and engaging ad copy that highlights the benefits of your products or services.
4. Use Eye-Catching Images: Use eye-catching images in your PPC ads to help them stand out and attract clicks.
5. Continuously Monitor and Refine Your Campaigns: Monitoring and refining your PPC advertising campaigns is key to achieving success and making the most of your advertising budget.

Optimizing Your PPC Campaigns for Lead Generation

1. Landing Page Optimization: Your landing page is the first thing potential customers will see when they click on your ad, so it's important to ensure it's optimized for lead generation. Ensure your landing page communicates the benefits of your products or services and provides a clear call to action for visitors.
2. Ad Group Structure: Ad group structure plays a critical role in the success of your PPC advertising campaigns. Create ad

groups around specific themes or products, and make sure your ad copy and keywords are aligned with each ad group's theme.

3. Bid Management: Bid management determines how much you're willing to pay for each click on your ad. To maximize your return on investment, continually monitor your bid prices and adjust them as needed based on the performance of your campaigns.

4. A/B Testing: A/B testing is a powerful tool for optimizing your PPC advertising campaigns. Test different elements of your campaigns, such as ad copy, images, and landing pages, to see what works best and make informed decisions about your advertising efforts.

5. Ad Extension Optimization: Ad extensions are additional information that can be added to your PPC ads, such as location, phone number, and more. Optimize your ad extensions to provide additional information to potential customers and increase the visibility and effectiveness of your ads.

Best Practices for PPC Advertising for Lead Generation

1. Adhere to Advertising Guidelines: Adhere to the advertising guidelines set forth by the platforms you're advertising on, such as Google Ads, to avoid penalties and ensure your ads are displayed correctly.

2. Use Relevant Keywords: Use relevant keywords in your PPC ads to increase their relevance and visibility to potential customers.

3. Regularly Monitor and Refine Your Campaigns: Regularly monitor and refine your PPC advertising campaigns to ensure they achieve your desired results and make the most of your advertising budget.
4. Use Mobile-Friendly Ad Designs: With most internet users accessing the web from mobile devices, it's important to ensure your PPC ads are optimized for mobile to reach the largest audience possible.
5. Test and Refine Your Ads Continuously: Test and refine your PPC ads continuously to identify what's working and what's not and make informed decisions about your advertising efforts.

PPC advertising is a powerful tool for lead generation that can help you reach specific audiences with relevant ads at the right time. By optimizing your campaigns and following best practices, you can achieve success with your PPC advertising efforts and drive more leads and sales for your business.

Chapter 11

Influencer Marketing

Introduction: Influencer marketing is a type of marketing that involves partnering with individuals who have a significant following on social media to promote your brand, products, or services. By leveraging the influence of these individuals, you can reach a large, engaged audience and generate interest in your brand.

Why Influencer Marketing Works: Influencer marketing works because people trust the opinions and recommendations of friends, family, and other trusted sources more than they trust traditional advertisements. When an influencer promotes a brand, their followers are more likely to trust their endorsement and be interested in learning more about the brand.

Choosing the Right Influencer: Choosing the right influencer is critical to the success of your influencer marketing campaign. Look for influencers with a strong, engaged following in your target market and whose values align with your brand. It's also important to choose influencers who have a genuine interest in your brand, products, or services and can effectively promote your brand to their followers.

Working with Influencers: When working with influencers, it's important to clearly define your objectives and goals for the campaign and to provide them with the information, materials, and resources they need to effectively promote your brand. Establish clear guidelines for the influencer, such as the type of content they should create and the frequency of their posts, and provide them with any product or service samples they need to create content.

Measuring the Success of Your Campaign: Measuring the success of your influencer marketing campaign's success is critical to determine your efforts' effectiveness and making informed decisions about future campaigns. Use metrics such as engagement rates, click-through rates, and sales to determine the success of your campaign, and use this information to make improvements for future campaigns.

Best Practices for Influencer Marketing: To get the most out of your influencer marketing efforts, follow these best practices:

1. Foster genuine relationships with influencers: Build genuine relationships with influencers by regularly interacting with them on social media and engaging with their content. This will help you establish trust and credibility with the influencer and make it more likely that they will promote your brand to their followers.
2. Be transparent: Be transparent with your influencer and their followers about the nature of your partnership. Ensure your brand's sponsorship or affiliation with the influencer is clearly stated in their content and related disclosures.
3. Provide value to the influencer's audience: Make sure the content you're promoting through the influencer provides value to their audience. This will help increase engagement rates and build credibility for your brand.

4. Measure and refine: Regularly measure the success of your influencer marketing campaigns and refine your approach as needed to maximize the impact of your efforts.
5. Be consistent: Make sure your brand's messaging and values are consistent across all of your influencer marketing campaigns. This will help build a strong, recognizable brand identity and make it easier for your audience to understand and connect with your brand.
6. Choose influencers who are a good fit: Not all influencers are a good fit for all brands, so choose influencers who are a good fit for your brand, products, or services. Look for influencers who share similar values and interests with your brand and who can promote your brand in a way that is authentic and engaging.
7. Use multiple influencers: Don't rely on just one influencer to promote your brand. Use multiple influencers to reach a wider audience and to ensure that your brand is being promoted to a diverse range of followers.
8. Offer incentives: Offering incentives, such as exclusive discounts or early access to new products, can help incentivize influencers to promote your brand and increase the impact of your influencer marketing efforts.
9. Be flexible: Be open to trying new things and experimenting with different approaches to see what works best for your brand. Influencer marketing is an evolving field, and being flexible and adaptable will help you stay ahead of the curve and achieve the best results.

10. Focus on long-term relationships: Building long-term relationships with influencers is key to the success of your influencer marketing efforts. Find ways to work with influencers on an ongoing basis and provide them with the support and resources they need to continue promoting your brand effectively.

Influencer marketing is a powerful tool for reaching a large, engaged audience and building interest in your brand. By choosing the right influencer, working closely with them, and following best practices, you can achieve great results with your influencer marketing efforts and drive more sales for your business.

Chapter 12

Event Marketing for Lead Generation

Define your goals: Before planning your event, define what you hope to achieve. Are you looking to generate new leads, build brand awareness, or drive sales? Having clear, measurable goals will help you create an event that is effective and impactful.

1. Choose the correct type of event: There are many different types of events, including trade shows, conferences, workshops, and product launches. Choose the type of event best suited to your goals, target audience, and brand image.
2. Choose the right venue: The venue you choose will have a significant impact on the success of your event. Consider factors such as location, accessibility, and the type of atmosphere you want to create when choosing a venue.
3. Plan your event carefully: Plan every aspect of your event carefully, from the type of food and drinks you will serve to the type of entertainment you will provide. Make sure you have a clear agenda and timeline and consider hiring a professional event planning team to help you create a successful event.
4. Promote your event: Use a variety of marketing channels to promote your event, including email, social media, and traditional advertising. Offer incentives, such as early bird discounts, to encourage people to register early.

5. Provide value: Make sure your event provides value to attendees by offering valuable content, educational sessions, and opportunities to network. Offer opportunities for attendees to interact with your brand, such as product demonstrations or hands-on workshops.
6. Collect leads: Make sure you have a process to collect leads and contact information from attendees. This can include setting up a lead generation booth, offering an incentive for attendees to provide their contact information, or using a lead capture tool like a tablet or mobile app.
7. Follow up: After the event, follow up with attendees to nurture your relationships and turn them into customers. Offer special discounts or promotions to attendees, and use the information you collected to personalize your follow-up communications.
8. Measure and evaluate your event: After the event, measure and evaluate its success. This can include tracking attendance, lead generation, and overall engagement. Use this information to make improvements for future events and to better understand the impact of your event marketing efforts.
9. Post-event engagement: Don't stop after the event; continue engaging with attendees and leads through email marketing, social media, and other marketing channels. Offer attendees access to exclusive content or promotions, and use the relationships you've built to move them further down the sales funnel.

10. Leverage technology: Utilize technology to make your event more engaging and effective. For example, use a mobile app to provide attendees with real-time updates, interactive features, and personalized schedules. You can also use social media to create a buzz around your event and keep attendees engaged even after the event.
11. Networking opportunities: Encourage attendees to network with one another and with your brand. Offer opportunities for attendees to connect with each other, such as roundtable discussions, break-out sessions, or after-event social events.
12. Personalization: Make your event feel personal to attendees. This can include offering personalized schedules, tailored content, or even a personalized gift or takeaway.
13. Continuously improve: Continuously evaluate your event marketing strategy and make improvements. Stay on top of industry trends, best practices, and customer feedback to ensure you're providing the best possible experience for your attendees.

By following these tips, you can create an event marketing strategy that is effective, engaging, and impactful. Whether you're a seasoned pro or just starting, event marketing can be a powerful tool for driving leads, building brand awareness, and nurturing relationships with customers.

Chapter 13

Trade Show Marketing

Define your goals: Before planning your trade show marketing strategy, define your goals. What do you hope to achieve from attending the trade show? Are you looking to generate leads, build brand awareness, or launch a new product? Having clear goals will help guide your trade show marketing efforts and ensure that you get the most out of your investment.

1. Research trade shows that are relevant to your industry and target audience. Look for trade shows that align with your goals and have a strong attendance rate.
2. Plan your booth: Your booth is your opportunity to make a lasting impression on attendees. Plan your booth layout, design, and messaging to make it visually appealing, inviting, and engaging.
3. Develop pre-show marketing: Pre-show marketing is an opportunity to build excitement and drive traffic to your booth. This can include email marketing, social media campaigns, and direct mail.
4. Offer something of value: Offer attendees something of value, such as a product demonstration, workshop, or giveaway. This will help attract attendees to your booth and give them a reason to engage with your brand.
5. Utilize social media: Utilize social media to build buzz and engage with attendees before, during, and after the trade

show. Use platforms like Twitter, Instagram, and LinkedIn to share updates, live videos, and photos from the event.
6. Follow-up with leads: After the trade show, follow up with leads to nurture relationships and move them further down the sales funnel. Email marketing, direct mail, or a personal phone call to keep the conversation going.
7. Measure and evaluate: After the trade show, measure and evaluate your results. This can include tracking lead generation, brand awareness, and overall engagement. Use this information to make improvements for future trade shows and to better understand the impact of your trade show marketing efforts.
8. Network and collaborate: Trade shows are also an opportunity to network and collaborate with other industry professionals and potential partners. Attend networking events, engage with other exhibitors, and seek opportunities to build relationships and expand your network.
9. Consider sponsorship opportunities: Consider sponsoring the trade show or a specific event or session. This can increase your brand visibility, provide opportunities to connect with attendees, and demonstrate your commitment to the industry.
10. Train your team: Prepare your team to represent your brand at the trade show. Provide training on your brand messaging, product knowledge, and how to engage with attendees. Ensure that your team is knowledgeable, friendly, and professional to make the most of your trade show investment.
11. Evaluate and adjust: Continuously evaluate and adjust your trade show marketing strategy as needed. Stay up-to-date on

industry trends, attend events and conferences to gather new ideas, and adapt your strategy based on your goals and results.

Trade show marketing can be a valuable tool for businesses looking to reach new customers, build brand awareness, and generate leads. By taking the time to plan and execute your strategy, you can maximize your return on investment and achieve your goals.

Chapter 14

Direct Mail Marketing

Introduction: Direct mail marketing is a targeted and personalized marketing approach that uses physical mail to reach customers. Direct mail can be an effective way to reach potential customers and build brand awareness. It can be used for a variety of purposes, including lead generation, customer engagement, and product promotion.

1. Define your target audience: To ensure that your direct mail campaign is effective, it's important to first define your target audience. Consider factors such as demographics, purchasing habits, and interests to create a targeted list of potential customers.

2. Choose the right format: Direct mail can take many forms, including postcards, letters, brochures, and catalogs. Choose the format that best suits your message and target audience.

3. Develop a clear call to Action: The main objective of your direct mail campaign should be to encourage recipients to take a specific action, such as visiting your website, signing up for a newsletter, or making a purchase. Make sure that your call to action is clear, concise, and easy to understand.

4. Make it personal: Personalizing your direct mail can help increase response rates and build customer relationships. Use the recipient's name, address, and other personal information to create a more personalized experience.

5. Test and refine: Test different elements of your direct mail campaign, such as the format, messaging, and call to action, to determine what works best. Continuously refine your approach based on your results to optimize your campaign over time.
6. Measure results: Track and measure the results of your direct mail campaign to understand its effectiveness. Consider metrics such as response rates, conversion rates, and ROI to assess the success of your efforts.
7. Integrate with other marketing efforts: Direct mail can be an effective complement to other marketing efforts, such as email marketing, social media, and events. Consider how direct mail can be integrated with these efforts to maximize the impact of your marketing campaigns.
8. Make it visually appealing: The design of your direct mail piece can greatly impact its effectiveness. Use visually appealing graphics, images, and typography to capture the recipient's attention and hold their interest.
9. Consider timing: Timing is critical for direct mail campaigns. Consider factors such as holidays, special events, and the recipient's buying cycle when deciding when to send your mail piece.
10. Comply with regulations: Direct mail is subject to various regulations, such as the CAN-SPAM Act, that govern how businesses can use mail for marketing purposes. Make sure that you comply with all relevant regulations to avoid legal issues and protect your reputation.

11. Keep it relevant: To maintain the recipient's interest, keep your direct mail relevant and up-to-date. Make sure that your content is current and addresses their needs and interests.
12. Use data to your advantage: Utilize data to optimize your direct mail campaign. Consider factors such as previous purchase history, website behavior, and demographic data to target your efforts and achieve better results.
13. Make it eco-friendly: Consider the environmental impact of your direct mail campaign by using eco-friendly materials, such as recycled paper and biodegradable envelopes, to minimize waste.
14. Conclusion: Direct mail can be an effective marketing tool when used properly. By following these best practices, you can create a successful direct mail campaign that helps you reach your marketing goals and build strong relationships with your customers.
15. Measure your results: One of the biggest advantages of direct mail is that it is easy to measure the results. Use response rates, conversion rates, and other metrics to evaluate the success of your campaign and make data-driven decisions for future efforts.
16. Continuously optimize: Direct mail is an ongoing process. Continuously evaluate and optimize your campaigns to improve your results and stay ahead of the competition. Consider testing different elements of your campaign, such as the call to action, and determine what resonates best with your audience.

17. Personalization: Personalization is key to direct mail success. Use the recipient's name, location, and other relevant information to make the message more personalized and appealing. This can increase response rates and help you build stronger relationships with your customers.
18. Target the right audience: Make sure that you are targeting the right audience for your direct mail campaign. Use demographic data, purchase history, and other relevant information to determine who is most likely to be interested in your products or services.
19. Test, test, test: Direct mail is a cost-effective way to reach your target audience, but it's important to test your campaign before launching it on a larger scale. Try out different formats, messaging, and targeting to see what works best for your business.
20. Create a sense of urgency: Use limited-time offers, exclusive promotions, and other tactics to create a sense of urgency and drive recipients to take action. This can help increase response rates and drive sales for your business.
21. Stay consistent: Direct mail is a long-term marketing strategy. Stay consistent in your messaging, branding, and overall approach to build brand recognition and establish yourself as a trusted source of information and products.

Direct mail marketing can be a valuable tool for businesses looking to reach potential customers and build brand awareness. By following these best practices, you can create an effective direct mail campaign that helps you achieve your marketing goals.

Chapter 15

Telemarketing and Cold Calling Techniques

Telemarketing and cold calling are two of the most direct and personal forms of marketing and sales tactics. These techniques allow you to connect directly with potential customers and engage them in conversation, making it a powerful tool for generating leads and closing sales. However, telemarketing and cold calling can also be difficult and challenging, as it requires a combination of effective communication, persuasive techniques, and an understanding of customer psychology. In this chapter, we will cover the basics of telemarketing and cold calling and provide tips and techniques for making these methods work for your business.

1. Understanding your audience: Before you make any calls, it's important to understand who your target audience is and what they are looking for. Use market research and customer data to identify the demographics, interests, and needs of your potential customers.

2. Developing a script: A script is a crucial element of successful telemarketing and cold calling. It should be well-written, concise, and tailored to your target audience. Make sure to include a clear opening, a compelling message, and a strong call to action.

3. Building rapport: Building rapport with potential customers is key to successful telemarketing and cold calling. Be friendly,

genuine, and interested in the person you are speaking with. Use active listening skills, ask questions, and make sure to tailor your conversation to the specific needs of each individual customer.

4. Overcoming objections: Objections are a natural part of the sales process, and they are an opportunity to build trust and rapport with your potential customers. Be prepared to handle common objections, such as price or competition, and use your persuasive skills to overcome them.

5. Closing the sale: The ultimate goal of telemarketing and cold calling is to close the sale. Use effective closing techniques, such as summarizing the benefits of your product or service, to persuade the customer to take action.

6. Managing rejections: Rejections are a part of telemarketing and cold calling, and it's important to be prepared to handle them with grace and professionalism. Use rejections as an opportunity to learn and improve your skills and stay positive and motivated.

7. Keeping track of your results: Telemarketing and cold calling is not just about making calls but also about measuring and analyzing your results. Use metrics, such as conversion rates and lead generation, to track your success and make data-driven decisions for future efforts.

8. Training and development: Telemarketing and cold calling are skills that can be improved with practice and training. Invest in the development of your telemarketing and cold calling skills, and continuously seek out opportunities to learn and grow.

When it comes to telemarketing, the key is to have a clear understanding of your target audience and to have a well-rehearsed script. You should have a clear understanding of the problem that your product or service solves and be able to articulate this in a way that is relevant to the person you are speaking to. Additionally, you should be able to identify the key benefits of your product or service and be able to clearly explain why your offering is the best solution for their needs.

Cold calling can be a bit more challenging, as you are reaching out to individuals who may not have shown an interest in your product or service. However, with the right approach, cold calling can be an effective way to generate leads and build your sales pipeline. The key is to be prepared, have a clear understanding of your target audience, and be persistent. You should also be familiar with common objections and be prepared to address them in a way that is both professional and persuasive.

One of the keys to success with telemarketing and cold calling is to have a well-designed follow-up system in place. This might include sending follow-up emails, making additional calls, or sending direct mail pieces. The goal is to keep your product or service top of mind and to build trust and credibility with your target audience over time.

Overall, telemarketing and cold calling can be extremely effective marketing and sales tactics, especially when done properly. By understanding your target audience, being well-prepared, and being persistent, you can generate leads, increase sales, and build your brand recognition.

Chapter 16

Sales Funnel Management

A sales funnel is the journey that a potential customer goes through, from initial awareness of a product or service to the final purchase. Understanding and managing the different stages of the sales funnel is essential to driving sales and growing your business.

The first stage of the sales funnel is awareness. This is where potential customers first become aware of your product or service. This can be through advertising, word of mouth, social media, or other marketing activities. The goal of this stage is to generate interest and attract potential customers to your website or landing page.

The next stage of the sales funnel is interest. At this stage, potential customers are actively seeking information about your product or service and evaluating whether it is the right solution for their needs. This is where you should provide educational content, such as blog posts, videos, webinars, and white papers, to help them make an informed decision.

The third stage of the sales funnel is desire. At this stage, potential customers have a clear understanding of the benefits of your product or service and are considering making a purchase. This is where you should focus on building desire by highlighting the key features and benefits of your product or service and offering special promotions or discounts to incentivize them to take action.

The final stage of the sales funnel is action. At this stage, potential customers are ready to make a purchase, and it's your job to make the process as seamless as possible. This might include offering multiple payment options, providing clear instructions, and providing excellent customer service.

To effectively manage your sales funnel, you need to have a clear understanding of the different stages and what activities are necessary to move potential customers from one stage to the next. You should also have a way to track and measure the effectiveness of your marketing and sales activities, so you can make improvements and optimize your sales funnel over time.

Overall, sales funnel management is a critical component of successful marketing and sales strategies. By understanding the different stages of the sales funnel and implementing the right activities to move potential customers through it, you can increase sales and grow your business.

To effectively manage your sales funnel, it's also important to segment your target audience based on their behavior and buying habits. This will allow you to tailor your marketing and sales activities to specific segments and increase the effectiveness of your efforts.

It's also important to continuously test and optimize your sales funnel to improve conversion rates. This can be done by A/B testing different elements, such as the copy on your landing page or the call-to-action (CTA) on your emails.

Another key aspect of sales funnels management is lead nurturing. Lead nurturing is the process of building relationships with potential customers who are not yet ready to make a purchase but are still interested in your product or service. By providing valuable content and building trust with these potential customers, you can keep them engaged and move them further down the sales funnel.

Additionally, it's important to have a clear understanding of the metrics and KPIs that are important for your sales funnel, such as conversion rates, lead-to-customer ratios, and average order value. By tracking these metrics, you can gain insights into what is working and what needs improvement and make data-driven decisions to optimize your sales funnel.

In conclusion, effective sales funnel management requires a clear understanding of the different stages of the sales funnel, a well-defined target audience, and a focus on testing, optimizing, and tracking results. By following these best practices, you can increase sales and grow your business.

Chapter 17

Closing Techniques for Sales

Closing a sale is the final and often most critical stage of the sales process. It's where the salesperson must effectively communicate the value of the product or service to the customer and address any objections they may have.

The following are some common closing techniques that can help increase the success rate of closing a sale:

1. The Assumptive Close: This technique assumes that the sale has already been made and asks the customer to confirm the details. For example, "Would you like the red or the blue option?"
2. The Alternative Close: This technique presents the customer with two options and asks them to choose. For example, "Would you like the standard package or the premium package?"
3. The Reverse Close: This technique involves asking the customer what would stop them from making a purchase. The salesperson can then address these concerns and overcome objections.
4. The Question Close: This technique involves asking the customer questions that lead them to the conclusion that they need the product or service. For example, "What do you think the benefits of this product will be for your business?"

5. The Summary Close: This technique involves summarizing the benefits of the product or service and asking the customer if they are ready to make a purchase.
6. The Takeaway Close: This technique involves making the sale conditional on some action by the customer, such as scheduling a follow-up call or visiting the store.

It's important to note that these techniques should be used as a tool and not relied upon solely. The best closing technique is one that is personalized to the customer and addresses their specific needs and concerns.

In addition to the techniques outlined above, it's important for sales professionals to have strong communication and interpersonal skills. Listening to the customer and understanding their needs and concerns is crucial in the closing process. Building rapport and establishing trust can also greatly improve the chances of closing a sale.

Another key factor in closing a sale is understanding the customer's buying process. This includes understanding their budget, decision-making process, and their timeline for making a purchase. By having this information, sales professionals can tailor their approach and messaging to meet the customer's specific needs.

Finally, it's important to stay positive and confident throughout the sales process, even if a customer does not immediately agree to make a purchase. Rejection is a normal part of the sales process and can provide valuable insights and feedback for future sales efforts.

In conclusion, closing techniques, strong communication skills, understanding the customer's buying process, and a positive and confident approach are all important components of the sales process. By incorporating these elements, sales professionals can increase their chances of successfully closing a sale.

Chapter 18

Building and Maintaining Customer Relationships

Building and maintaining customer relationships is an essential aspect of successful sales and marketing. A strong relationship with a customer not only leads to repeat business but can also result in positive word-of-mouth promotion and increased referral business.

The first step in building a customer relationship is to understand the customer's needs and preferences. This can be accomplished through regular communication and feedback sessions, as well as by analyzing customer data. This information can be used to tailor the company's products, services, and marketing messages to meet the specific needs of each customer.

In order to maintain a strong customer relationship, it's important to provide excellent customer service. This includes being responsive to customer inquiries and concerns, resolving any issues in a timely manner, and consistently delivering high-quality products and services.

Building customer loyalty can be achieved through various initiatives such as rewards programs, exclusive events, and personalized offers. By making customers feel valued and appreciated, companies can strengthen their relationships with their customers and increase customer retention.

It's also important to consistently evaluate and adjust the customer relationship strategy based on customer feedback and changing market conditions. By staying adaptable and proactive, companies can ensure that their customer relationships remain strong and mutually beneficial.

In addition to the above, companies can also establish long-term customer relationships by going above and beyond their expectations. This can include offering additional value-added services, such as training, support, and consultation. Companies can also differentiate themselves by providing unique, personalized experiences that are tailored to each customer's needs and preferences.

It's also important to maintain open and transparent communication with customers. Regular updates on new products, services, and promotions, as well as surveys and feedback sessions, can help companies stay connected with their customers and gain valuable insights into their needs and preferences.

Another key aspect of building customer relationships is building trust. Companies can build trust by consistently delivering on their promises, being transparent about their operations, and demonstrating a commitment to ethical business practices.

Finally, companies can also leverage technology to build and maintain customer relationships. For example, using customer relationship management (CRM) software can help companies organize customer data, track customer interactions, and automate follow-up tasks. Additionally, social media can be used to engage with customers, respond to inquiries and concerns, and share company news and promotions.

In conclusion, building and maintaining customer relationships is a complex and ongoing process. By taking a strategic approach that includes understanding customer needs, providing excellent customer service, building customer loyalty, maintaining open communication, building trust, leveraging technology, and consistently evaluating and adjusting their approach, companies can establish long-lasting, mutually beneficial relationships with their customers.

Chapter 19

Measuring and Analyzing Marketing and Sales Performance

In today's highly competitive business environment, companies must continually evaluate and optimize their marketing and sales strategies to ensure they are delivering the desired results. Measuring and analyzing performance enables companies to identify areas of strength and weakness and make informed decisions about how to adjust their approach to improve results.

Measuring Marketing Performance: To measure marketing performance, companies must first establish clear and specific marketing objectives. This could include goals such as increasing brand awareness, generating leads, or driving sales. Once objectives have been established, companies can use a variety of tools and metrics to measure their performance, including:

- Website analytics: This measures website traffic, including the number of visitors, time spent on the site, and conversion rates.
- Social media analytics: This measures engagement on social media platforms, including likes, shares, and comments.
- Email marketing metrics: This measures the effectiveness of email campaigns, including open rates, click-through rates, and conversion rates.
- Influencer marketing metrics: This measures the impact of influencer marketing campaigns, including reach, engagement, and conversions.

- Content marketing metrics: This measures the success of content marketing efforts, including views, shares, and conversions.

Measuring Sales Performance: To measure sales performance, companies can use a variety of metrics, including:

- Sales volume: This measures the total number of sales made.
- Average sale value: This measures the average value of each sale.
- Conversion rate: This measures the percentage of sales opportunities that result in a sale.
- Sales cycle time: This measures the length of time it takes to close a sale.
- Customer acquisition cost: This measures the cost of acquiring each new customer.

Analyzing Marketing and Sales Performance: Once data has been collected, companies can analyze their performance to identify areas of strength and weakness. This can include analyzing:

- Trends: This identifies patterns and trends in performance over time.
- Comparisons: This compares performance to industry benchmarks and previous periods.
- Root causes: This identifies the underlying causes of performance, such as changes in consumer behavior or market conditions.

Using this information, companies can make informed decisions about how to adjust their marketing and sales strategies to improve results. This could include adjusting their target audience, refining their messaging, or investing in new marketing channels.

In order to effectively evaluate the success of your marketing and sales efforts, it is crucial to establish clear, measurable goals and track your progress over time. This will help you to identify areas that need improvement, as well as to understand what strategies are working well for your business.

There are a variety of metrics that can be used to measure the success of your marketing and sales activities. For example, you might track the number of website visitors, the number of leads generated, the conversion rate of leads to customers, and the lifetime value of each customer. Additionally, you might track the return on investment (ROI) of your various marketing and sales activities to determine which is providing the highest return for your investment of time and resources.

One important aspect of measuring and analyzing your marketing and sales performance is to identify trends over time. By monitoring your metrics on a regular basis, you can determine whether your efforts are resulting in consistent growth or whether there are fluctuations that require further investigation. This information can help you to make informed decisions about the future direction of your business and how to allocate your resources most effectively.

Another important aspect of measuring and analyzing your marketing and sales performance is to compare your results with industry benchmarks. This can help you to see how you are performing in comparison to other businesses in your industry and to identify areas where you may be able to improve.

Ultimately, the goal of measuring and analyzing your marketing and sales performance is to gain a deeper understanding of your customers and to optimize your efforts to reach and engage them effectively. By continually monitoring your results and making data-driven decisions, you can ensure that your marketing and sales activities are driving growth and success for your business.

Chapter 20

Staying Up-to-Date with Marketing and Sales Trends

Marketing and sales strategies are constantly evolving, and it is important to stay informed about the latest trends and developments in order to remain competitive and effective in your efforts. This can be achieved through ongoing education and professional development, as well as by staying engaged with industry thought leaders and experts.

One way to stay up-to-date with marketing and sales trends is to attend conferences and workshops, where you can learn from experts in the field and network with other professionals. You can also stay informed by reading industry publications, such as trade magazines and blogs, and following thought leaders on social media. Additionally, you can participate in online discussion forums and attend webinars to expand your knowledge and gain insights from experts.

Another important aspect of staying up-to-date with marketing and sales trends is to continuously evaluate and adjust your strategies based on your results and industry trends. This requires a commitment to testing and experimenting with new techniques and approaches, as well as staying aware of new technologies and tools that can help you to reach and engage your target audience more effectively.

In addition to staying up-to-date with marketing and sales trends, it is also important to remain vigilant about changes in the marketplace and your industry. This can include monitoring competitor activities, tracking changes in customer behavior and preferences, and paying attention to broader economic and technological trends that may impact your business.

Ultimately, staying up-to-date with marketing and sales trends requires a proactive and continuous effort to educate yourself, test new ideas, and stay informed about changes in your industry and the marketplace. By doing so, you can ensure that your marketing and sales strategies are always relevant and effective, driving growth and success for your business.

The key to staying up-to-date with marketing and sales trends is to make a commitment to ongoing learning and development. This requires a proactive and continuous effort to educate yourself, test new ideas, and stay informed about changes in your industry and the marketplace. By being open to new ideas and approaches, you can remain innovative and effective in your marketing and sales efforts, helping your business to stay ahead of the curve and achieve success.

Additionally, it is important to not just focus on staying up-to-date with trends but also to continuously analyze and measure the performance of your marketing and sales efforts. This can help you to identify areas for improvement and adjust your strategies accordingly, ensuring that your marketing and sales efforts are always aligned with your business goals and driving the best possible results.

By embracing a culture of continuous learning and development and by staying informed about the latest trends and developments in marketing and sales, you can ensure that your efforts are always effective and aligned with your business goals. With this approach, you can drive growth, engagement, and success for your business, both now and in the future.

In conclusion, marketing and sales are two critical components of any successful business. They play a vital role in attracting and retaining customers, building brand awareness, and driving growth and revenue. Whether you are just starting out or are a seasoned professional, the tactics and strategies outlined in this book can help you to create a comprehensive and effective marketing and sales plan that will drive results for your business.

By understanding your target audience, developing a marketing strategy, building a strong brand identity, leveraging digital marketing channels, and focusing on customer relationships, you can create a winning formula for success. And by continually measuring and analyzing your performance and staying up-to-date with the latest trends and developments, you can ensure that your marketing and sales efforts are always aligned with your business goals and driving the best possible outcomes.

With this book as your guide, you have the tools and knowledge you need to succeed. So go forth and conquer the world of marketing and sales, and watch your business grow and thrive!

www.ingramcontent.com/pod-product-compliance
Lightning Source LLC
Chambersburg PA
CBHW050241220526
45465CB00017B/724